T0277499

Emotions 2 Words
Second Edition

For more information, please contact:
Silk Rhode Books
868 Greenville Ave
Johnston, RI 02919
silkrhodebooks@gmail.com

LCCN: 2023950804
ISBN: 978-1-7370446-8-0

Illustrations by
KD Lawrence & Jason Pagano

This book is dedicated to my daughter,
Kara J. Lawrence.
I love you deeply, Little Mini Me.
Express your pain. It helps!

In loving memory of
Mary Ellen Borghatti, my best friend.
Your friendship helped me create this book.
You are truly missed.

Acknowledgments

First, I would like to thank God for inspiring me to be a writer when I was in deep emotional pain. Writing became my best girlfriend through all the drama in my life.

I would like to thank my mother for standing by me when no one else would and loving me when no one else could. Mom, you give me inspiration every single day.

To my children, Kendrick, Kara, and Karli (Max), I love you so much.

Thanks so much for supporting Mommy, and understanding "Mommy Time."

You are the best kids a single mom could ever have. Thank you for forcing me to finish and publish this work.

Emotions 2 Words

KD Lawrence

I Cried

I cried,
when I saw my Aunt died.
Cancer tears flowed
from her beautiful eyes.

I cried,
when I caught my man in a lie.
The truth was there in his open fly.

I cried,
when my daughter was born;
Remember, you were in ATL
watching porn.

I cried,
until 4 o'clock in the morning;
Up came the sun and
in came my learning.

Boy, did I cry
when they took my car.
Money stopped coming in, no credit,
no job, times were hard.

I'm taking care of our little star.
While Daddy sits at the bar.

I cried,
like a baby when I felt so used.
You lied and cheated,
I couldn't take your abuse.

I cried,
on the floor after the fight.
You hit me, I screamed,
Police came; that ain't right.

After every tear I cried,
You could never tell me the truth;
an expert liar and I wasn't your muse.

James

I hear you calling my name;
   Why are you trying to run game?
I see you on the corner
   still doing the same.
I know you see me
   because you answered to "James."

When I first met you,
   you were the man of my dreams.
Heaven only knew one day
   you would make me scream.

Tonight, as I see the
   passion in your eyes,
Lord knows what you have down there
   took me by surprise.

With all your class
   and flashy clothes
No one would ever guess
you couldn't afford
   to buy me a rose —

— or even take me out.
Guess that's not what
   you're all about.

You treat women like toys;
brag and boast
   to your boys.

If they ever found out,
You would lose
   your clout.

If You Look In My Heart

If you look in my heart,
  you will see love
    that never runs cold.

If you look in my heart,
  you will find secrets
    inside my soul.

If you touch my heart,
  you will feel
    passion and love.

If you touch my heart,
  you will find
    the warmth of a dove.

If you speak to my heart,
  you will not
    find race.

If you speak to my heart,
  you will know
    my taste.

If you look in my heart,
  you will see
    pain and sorrow.

If you look in my heart,
  you'll love me today
    and not tomorrow.

If you listen to my heart,
  it will say
    "I Love You."

Pain

It turns your heart inside out.
You sit and wonder
what this pain is all about.

You can't eat or sleep,
you lay awake all night.
You want to scream or yell,
maybe even fight.

You cry all day and night,
lying in your bed like a baby.
You asked if he loved you and
he said "maybe".

Your stomach turns
and your body feels numb.
Food tastes like dust
you just feel so dumb.

You pace the floor or sit by the door,
"How can he do this to me,"
you ask and implore.

The calls come in
from others, not him.
He avoids you like the plague.

In your head, the voices
singing of his choices —
those awful things he said —
then wishing he was dead.

Cold

He left me, it was so cold.
I cried, cause it's so old.
Now the whole world knows.
The pain, the guilt, everyone knows.

Deep inside, I want to move on.
I realize this man has a son.
Somebody grab
   my hand from the gun.
Take me away, I can't stand.

I don't know how this mess began.
I thought he was my man.
I don't want to start again.
Yet, I feel this is the end.
Another Woman!

How can I be your friend?
You left me, this is the END.

I need to move on,
   so I can breathe again.

Please let me go
   so I can feel again.

You Me Too

When you said,
"I love you."
I said,
"Me Too."

When you hold me,
I say, "Me Too."

Whispering our future in my ear,
My heart says, "Me Too."

Working with my babe,
Together forever,
My lover, my partner,
My friend says, "Me Too."

As you caress my body,
You touch me, "Me Too."

Strolling along the common,
You hold my hand,
you want me, "Me Too."
Cross the table you glance,
My foot touches you,
I see it in your eyes,
You want, "Me Too."

We make love, you hold me,
My girl says, "Me Too."

You are my number one,
 I am your earth,
You are my sun,
Together we are a Universe!
God sees us in love, "You Me Too."

The Perfect Day

Wake up in the morning,
  glanced out my window.
The sun is shining with gleam,
  as far as the eye can see.
Push off my covers
  and puff my pillows.
This is going to be
  the Perfect Day for me.

Eat, get dressed,
  my hair in a mess.
I jump in my jeans and a tee,
  I guess
Make sure my makeup looks great.
I don't want to be late.
  Today, I have a date!

Some cat, named Jack,
  I met a few years back.
Damn, I think I need to pack.
We're spending the whole weekend
  in the sack.

He likes to paint my toes.
It's a secret no one knows.
He makes me breakfast
   and feeds me dinner.
He said, let's get married.
You're a winner...

He makes me laugh,
   I even blush and smile.
Is this a crush, real love?
I'll just chill for a while.

We lay and wait for dinner to bake.
I can't wait to eat
   some wedding cake.

It will be a special day,
   I think in May.
Everyone will say,
   "This is the Perfect Day!"

Peace

Be Still

Sitting by the window;
    watching the rain.
Thinking about my life,
    the joy and pain.

Reflecting over the past thirty years.
Asking the Lord,
    "How did I get here?"

I'm scared 'cause this road
    doesn't seem clear.
My prayers to the Lord seem
    to fall on deaf ears.

The Reverend said,
    "The Devil is busy."
I am trapped in a mess and
    my life's in a tissy.

The thunder is roaring and
   I opened my Bible
   to see the words
   "Peace Be Still."
What does this mean?

Young people say "chill".
The doctors put me on
   all kinds of them pills.
Lawyer told me to write a will.
Mama said,
   "I think you might be ill."

The Lord touched me and said,
   "You don't need the pills,
   because you are not ill."

Your Father has heard you,
   "Peace Be Still."

Accept Me

Accept me, as I am.
I can be a Diva
   and I can get glam.

In your eyes,
   I should be your world.
Our vision together
   has brought us a little girl.

My life with you became hectic.
I use to lie in bed at night
   alone, naked.

You had friends who needed you
   back then.
I had men that wanted me
   to be their woman.

You could never see things that I see.
I thought you loved me,
    but you couldn't understand me.
I turned into your worst nightmare.
Yet, so many nights I wanted you here.

I cried and prayed
    for you to come home.
You left the family all alone
    without a phone.

I am trying to rebuild
    and get me back together.
Then, one day I open the mail
    and there was a letter.

Now you want me to understand;
She's in your life.
For the very first time you talked
about her as "My soon to be wife."

You tell me,
  "I just don't want to fight."
A kiss on the cheek
  and you say good night.

After hearing this news,
  I could not stand.
No one to love me,
  nor hold my hand;
I am going out to the club
  to find me a new man.

We can do it too.
Can't you see
    we know this game too?

This is my life.
    I got faith.
One day you will
    feel my pain.

I am one wild horse
    you can't tame.
She'll see you're not real,
    you're a damn shame.

Our child doesn't even
    know your name.
Next time I see you,
    I'll treat you the same.

Secret Child

My eyes met yours in a crowded club;
Within three weeks
    you told me it was love.
You told me you wanted me
    to have your baby.
I never knew you had another lady.

We kicked it for months
    then you proposed.
We planned to have a wedding.
Photographer, cake, music,
    and venue were all set.
One thing I guess you tried to forget.

You have another!

Our child-to-be has a brother.
You gonna make me a baby's mother.
Wait til I tell yo' mother...

You Believed In Me

When my days were dark
  and the nights were cold.
Hours would pass and the ship
  just would not seem to dock.

You believed in me...

The tides rolled
  and the waves were tossed.
I was lost
  and there was no light but a spark.

You believed in me...

Your faith in me gave me a start.
I opened up
  to give the Lord my heart.

You believed in me...

Your voice seemed to set me straight.
You said,
  "Love the Lord. It is never too late".

You believed in me...

In a few conversations,
   you put me on a path.
You made me remember
   how to laugh.

You believed in me...

The world is evil and someone
   has messed with God's child.
You told me to fight and now
   I am proud.

You believed in me...

I had faith and I believed
   one day I would be set free.
With you and God by my side
   these worries of the world
   would have to let me be.

Because, both of You believed in me.

Dedicated to Judy Lawrence (Mom)

Lord, Send Me a Man

I met this man but
    he was not my type.
I am hoping one day,
    I can get this right.

The men I meet
    aren't on the same path.
Some drug dealers, liars,
    lost souls, or cheaters -
    you find out in the aftermath.

I need someone to share my time.
I am settled, together,
    and I think I look fine.

Help me to meet that special one.
With your blessing, maybe,
    we could have a son.

Send me someone
    to share my dreams.
No more fighting,
    yelling, or arguing.

I want him to put a smile on my face
when he enters a room.
He makes me proud
    to have him as my groom.

Give me the man you think I need,
    even though I have
    my own wants and desires.

A man who believes in
    your power and love;

Just as I do.

Lord, please send me a man
    in the image of you.